BRADFORD AS IT WAS

by

Gary Firth

Front cover: Market Street at the turn of the century.

First Edition May 1978.
Second impression December 1983.

Published by Hendon Publishing Company Limited, Hendon Mill, Nelson, Lancashire.
Text © Gary Firth, 1978.

Printed by Fretwell & Brian Ltd., Goulbourne St., Keighley, West Yorkshire, BD21 1PZ.

Introduction

As a Welfare State baby, the majority of photographs in this collection are beyond my ken and yet I am still close to much of the atmosphere and texture of pre-war Bradford. This close affinity, even kinship, has grown out of the many hours of conversation with my grandparents, particularly grandad. A master of the anecdote, and ever mindful of the past, the streets, characters and events of inter-war Bradford have come alive through his colourful and accurate evocation of the past. To him more than anyone else I should like to dedicate this publication.

The bulk of the photographs fall into that fifty years after 1870 when Yorkshire's textile capital was threatened by a prolonged recession of its staple trade. As profits fell, mills and even ironworks closed and strikes were the fruitless reactions to falling living standards. Yet the new century marked a more positive beginning in municipal welfare and responsibility. Much of what Sir Titus Salt had intended for Bradford, and had realised at Saltaire, was earnestly attempted in this period. Municipal housing, clinics, hospitals, schools and colleges and a whole range of public services were introduced in these years and did much to improve the quality of life for Bradfordians. They went some way towards softening the blows of the Great War and its disastrous economic consequences for our region. It is hoped the following pages conjure up some of the character, spirit and humour of Bradford in this eventful period.

Several of the photographs in this publication have come from the collection in the Local History Library, Bradford Central Library and I should like to thank Miss Wilmott for permission to use them. My thanks are also due to the Bradford Telegraph and Argus for permission to draw upon their photographic archives. Some photographs are from private collections and I am grateful to Mabel G. Bruce; Kenneth Young and Stephen Roberts. My acknowledgements to Lund Humphries and to the publishers of the I.L.P. Jubilee Souvenir 1893-1943. Finally, grateful thanks to Alan Thompson for invaluable photographic assistance and to Hilda Watkinson for typing the text.

G. Firth.
December, 1977.

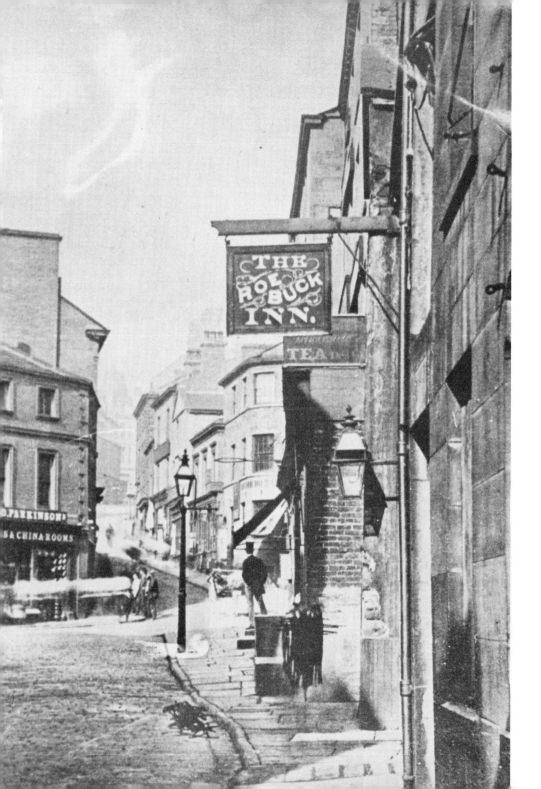

1. LOOKING UP IVEGATE, c1860. One of Bradford's oldest highways, Ivegate's status had deteriorated by 1850. Shoppers and retailers ignored it because of its steepness and narrowness and few improvements were made to its ancient character in Victorian times. This very old photograph was taken outside the Roebuck Inn, headquarters of the union in the great Woolcombers and Weavers Strike of 1825. David Parkinson lost his life in a fire at the china shop shown on the left. Further up the street on the right, is the Unicorn Hotel, a well known music hall for amateur comedians and singers. The main features of Ivegate since 1840 have been its pubs and pork shops and it was to these that the young men of the town were attracted for a good Saturday night out.

2. Top left. OLD TALBOT HOTEL, KIRKGATE, c1880. In the early decades of the nineteenth century this ancient hostelry was the headquarters of the Bradford Tories and was patronised by such famous 'blues' as E. C. Lister and Frank Duffield. It was one of the town's great coaching houses, the 'Union' calling here daily on its runs from Leeds to Kendal. The hotel was considerably rebuilt in 1879/80.

3. Bottom left. LAYING OF THE FOUNDATION STONE, BRADFORD TOWN HALL 1870. The Bradford Council, in 1870, finally accepted the tender of John Ives & Son of Shipley for the new town hall building. A month later, the foundation stone was laid amid great ceremony. Local dignitaries, headed by the Mayor, Alderman Mark Dawson, marched in procession to the site which was surrounded by platforms, barriers and an enormous gallery on the Chapel Lane side, all full of people. The Mayor laid the foundation stone (north east corner of the tower) with a silver gilt trowel presented to him by Matthew Thompson.

4. Right. INSTALLATION OF 'MATTHEW WILLIAM' 1873. This four ton bell, named after Bradford's Mayor Matthew William Thompson, was installed for the opening of the Town Hall in September, 1873. A carillon machine with three barrels enabled Bradfordians to hear a different tune each day for three weeks. The total cost of all the bells and the clock was £4,013.

5. Top left. BRADFORD MOOR BARRACKS 1870. It was here that a company of the 5th Dragoon Guards was stationed throughout the 1840's when physical-force Chartism was at its height in the area. In the half century after 1884 the barracks were occupied successively by the Green Howards, 70th West Riding Brigade Royal Artillery and the Royal Army Service Corps. The site of the barracks is now occupied by the premises of a large engineering company.

6. Bottom left. JOHN O' JUDY, c1860. Near Norwood Green in the parish of North Bierley is Horse Close Bridge. To Bradfordians of the mid-Victorian age it was better known as 'Judy Brig', named after 'Gurt Judy' the second wife of Joseph North. This portly dame had a son to an earlier marriage who was well known as John o' Judy's to the many summer picnic parties which visited the public gardens under Joseph Nutter's supervision. Here, John o' Judy is examining the intricacies of a camera at Judy Gardens where he died in March 1869.

7. Left. JOHN WOOD. Born in 1793 John Wood entered the Bradford worsted trade at the age of nineteen setting up his own combing and spinning business. Within twenty years he was the town's largest employer. He ran a factory school for 500 children and financed many local charities. As an Anglican Tory he was a founding father of the 10 Hour Movement. His fortune made, Wood gradually handed on his business to his half cousin William Walker. By 1855 John Wood had bought himself into the ranks of the Hampshire squirearchy. This photograph was taken shortly before his death in 1871.

8. Top left. NEWLANDS MILL CHIMNEY FALL, 1882. This was the scene of Bradford's worst disaster on a site between Ripley Street and Upper Castle Street, off Manchester Road. For some days before the fall there had been fears that it was in danger of collapsing. It fell at nine o'clock on the morning of 28th December 1882. Most of the mill occupants had just settled down to their breakfasts. In addition to the seventy injured, fifty-three bodies were taken from the devastated area over the six days following the disaster. Many of them were teenage mill girls whose parents had great difficulty in identifying them.

9. Bottom left. MANOR HALL, c1878. The ravages of Bradford's nineteenth century urban growth have taken their toll on the grandeur of this fine building. Erected in 1705 in Kirkgate, it was formerly enclosed by gardens and fields with an extensive orchard at the rear. By 1825 it was surrounded by the new Market Place with its retailers, hawkers and characters like Tommy Ramsden and Tom Hardy, advocates of temperance appealing to the crowds on Saturday nights. By 1875 the building had become an eating house and temperance hotel. The site was later cleared and the former Kirkgate Market went up.

10. Right. 'OLD CROWN', IVEGATE 1906. A very ancient hostelry in Ivegate, the Old Crown was renowned for its tiny rooms, low ceilings and its narrow corridors. In the nineteenth century it offered accommodation to those who were not too fussy about home comforts. Its reputation was not enhanced when it later became a music hall. In this photograph William Richardson stands at the door of the dram shop which he had converted out of a window corner. On the right is Tommy Wardle's, retailer of pans, kettles, fenders, scuttles, baths and fire irons.

11. Top left. 'TAWS'. A break for two Bradford errand boys at the turn of the century. They are playing taws, marbles or glass alleys. Most boys of the lower classes held part time jobs long before they left school. As unofficial errand boys they gathered round railway and omnibus stations, telegraph offices and large hotels. They fetched and carried for building labourers, mill workers and foundrymen. They were abused and exploited by a few employers but the majority of these lads earned important shillings for the family income, sometimes treating themselves to a copy of 'Magnet', 'Gem' or 'Union Jack'.

12. Botton left. WAIFS OF THE BRADFORD CHURCH SCHOOL, 1908. It was children like these, who were rescued by the progressive social work of Margaret McMillan. In Bradford Board Schools she found children in every stage of neglect and dirt and suffering. The situation in the city's voluntary schools, like the Parish Church School, was no better. Bradford's first school medical inspection was held at Usher Street School in 1899. By 1908 three and a half thousand Bradford schoolchildren were being inspected annually by the city's medical staff.

13. Right. ADVERTISING IN FORSTER SQUARE. Before the age of the commercial break, stores advertised themselves and their goods in a variety of ways. John S. Driver, general grocer and greengrocer certainly goes to great lengths in this pre 1914 sales campaign. From their headquarters in Ingleby Road and their numerous branches around Bradford, John S. Driver supplied cheap but quality goods. During the hard times of the inter-war years, thousands were thankful for the 'Driver Parcel' of rabbit, one onion, a carrot, small turnip and a few potatoes, all for a shilling!

14. Far left. THE SALT STATUE, 1888. The statue had pride of place in front of the new town hall until it caused traffic congestion in the 1890's. It was erected in Salt's lifetime, as a tribute from the people of Bradford and Saltaire. A public holiday was declared when it was unveiled by the Duke of Devonshire in 1874. It was moved to Lister Park in the summer of 1896.

15. Top left. PEEL SQUARE, c1890. Peel's statue was an expression of gratitude from Bradford's men of commerce for the free trade policy implemented by that statesman. Surrounded by the profusely carved warehouses of 'New Germany' the statue was unveiled in November 1855 in the presence of the sculptor, William Behnes. Since 1957 the statue has been located in Peel Park. The photograph shows the junction of Leeds Road (left of statue) and Hall Ings.

16. Bottom left. PACKING DEPARTMENT OF A BRADFORD MILL, c1910. In 1901 over 57,000 Bradfordians were employed in textile manufacture. The majority of women worked in the spinning and weaving departments of the city's mills. Sorting, combing and dyeing chiefly employed men. Before 1914, Bradford is thought to have handled, in some way or other, five sixths of the wool in this country. Every wool transaction, from exporting the raw material to retailing the finished piece, was dealt with in Bradford. In 1910, the City's annual turnover in textiles was estimated at ninety million pounds.

17. Top right. THE SPOTTED HOUSE, 1895. The old farmhouse was originally part of the Lister estate at Manningham and in 1811 one of only four houses along Manningham Low Lane. The photograph shows distinctly the extension of the original house to adjoin the main Keighley-Bradford turnpike road (1825). This wing was added by E. C. Lister of Manningham Hall and served as his justice room for the regular petty sessions. Known formerly as the Lister's Arms (1840) its status was raised above that of the common drinking house by John Boyes Tankard after 1870. By the time of his death in 1894 the hostelry had its own bowling green, tennis court and swimming pool and had become, according to one contemporary, 'a suburban house of refreshment'.

18. Bottom right. BRADFORD STREET BAND, c1890. Such bands brought a welcome break to the hum-drum of street life. Though their music was not of the highest standard, they provided a gaiety, and a chance for young and old to let their hair down in communal sing-songs, even dancing.

19. Left. PETER BUSSEY. One of the earliest leaders of the labour movement in Bradford was Peter Bussey (born 1805). The son of a Bedale draper, he moved into the Bradford worsted trade as a woolcomber. Leader of the Bradford Political Union in 1831, an advocate of factory reform and branch secretary of Owen's Grand National Consolidated Trade Union in 1834, Bussey served a full apprenticeship for physical force Chartism in 1838-40. His failure to lead the Northern rising meant his disgrace and subsequent escape to America where he became a street hawker. He returned to England in 1854 and died fifteen years later.

A PICNIC GROUP AFTER BEN TILLETT'S CANDIDATURE FOR BRADFORD W. 1892
Extreme right—Ben Turner (delegate at 1893 Conference) and Mrs. Turner.
Centre—Mrs. Jowett, F. W. Jowett, Mrs. Tillett (with child), Ben Tillett.
On ground at left—W. H. Drew.

20. Top left. BEN TILLETT'S PICNIC GROUP. The Manningham Mills strike of 1891 precipitated the working men of Bradford into creating a political organisation of their own, the Bradford Labour Union. Unlike the Labour Electoral Association this new body refused to work within the Liberal party and put forward their own candidate, Ben Tillett, for Bradford West in the general election of 1892. Tillett ran a creditable third but the Labour Union (renamed Bradford Independent Labour Party) had been established as a positive political force. Here, Tillett, his family and supporters relax during the election campaign.

THE FIRST NATIONAL COUNCIL OF THE I.L.P.
Back Row (left to right)—A. Field, J. Kennedy, J. Lister (Treasurer).
Row (left to right)—G. S. Christie, J. W. Buttery, Joseph Burgess, W. H. Drew, F. Axelme, Alf. Settle

21. Bottom left. FORMATION OF I.L.P. IN BRADFORD 1893. The success of the Bradford Labour Union in 1892 confirmed its leadership of the labour movement and Bradford was consequently the venue of the inaugural conference of the national party in January 1893. In the photograph the newly elected national council of the Independent Labour Party stands before the Labour Institute in Peckover Street. Shaw Maxwell, former chairman of the Scottish Labour Party was elected secretary and John Lister of Shibden Hall, Halifax, became treasurer.

22. Left. JUBILEE FIRE, HORTON, 1897. This enormous pile at Revey Beacon was the City of Bradford's Municipal Jubilee bonfire. Queen Victoria's Diamond Jubilee coincided with the golden jubilee of Bradford's status as a municipality. The Council, mindful of the town's phenomenal growth in the intervening years, petitioned the Queen to raise Bradford to the rank of a city. Thus Bradfordians had cause to enjoy a double celebration in the summer of 1897.

23. Top left. CORONATION CELEBRATIONS, NORWOOD GREEN, 1902. The Victorian age ended 22nd January 1901 with the death of the old queen. King Edward's coronation was postponed until the summer of 1902, owing to his illness. Norwood Green's coronation celebrations took place on Saturday 9th August of that year, when a procession of school-children and the Parish Council were accompanied to Field Head Farm by the Brighouse and Raistrick Temperance Brass Band. The children of the village enjoyed side-shows and rides on two decorated motor cars. They were given coronation mugs; followed by an enormous bunfight at the School. In the evening their parents roasted a sheep and toasted the health of the new king. The Edwardian era had begun.

24. Bottom left. SOMALI VILLAGE, BRADFORD EXHIBITION, 1904. The aged Lord Masham had officially opened the Cartwright Memorial Hall in April 1904. The Inaugural Exhibition commenced 4th May of that year and was opened by the Prince and Princess of Wales (afterwards King George V and Queen Mary). One of the many highlights of the exhibition was a real Somali village inhabited by natives of that country. For months they were continuously a public spectacle, several of their huts burnt down and a number of them died in this strange land.

25. Left. THE VICTORIA STATUE. Later the Prince and Princess of Wales returned to Bradford for the unveiling of Queen Victoria's statue. A gallery had been specially erected for the occasion and three thousand Bradford school children sang for the royal guests. Brilliant sunshine, the colour and noise of military bands, brought 50,000 Bradfordians into the city centre that day. Backcloth to the photograph is the Horton Lane Congregational Chapel.

26. Top right. NEW WESLEYAN CHAPEL AND SCHOOL, WESTGATE HILL 1903. Westgate Hill, between Tong and Dudley Hill, had a long connection with Wesleyan Methodism. The first chapel had been built there in 1800. Whilst the Boer War raged, the trustees decided to build a new chapel and Sunday School, and in 1902 the former, with its elegant spire, was completed. A year later, 26th August 1903 (here in this photograph) the local bene-factor James Oddy of Moorland Hall, Birkenshaw, opened the Sunday Schools.

27. Bottom right. THE WESLEYAN CHARIOT, 1905. Rev. H. M. Nield of Eastbrook Hall pioneered this portable pulpit for his open-air gospel work. Successful missionary work was conducted at weekly meetings in Morley Street and in front of the Bradford Exchange. The open-air Temperance Crusade of 1905 was so effective that several Bradford publicans demanded a revision of their poor rates on the grounds that 'the Eastbrook Brotherhood had robbed them of their customers'.

28. Top left. EASTBROOK BROTHERHOOD. The Eastbrook Brotherhood became the model for Men's Meetings everywhere after its foundation by Rev. H. M. Nield in September 1904. Nield's successor in 1911 was Rev. G. G. Muir and in spite of the war, the Brotherhood continued to thrive. Muir attracted to the Brotherhood many celebrated speakers including A. Conan Doyle, Lord Bishop of Bradford, Gypsy Smith and here in this photograph Rt. Hon. Arthur Henderson prepares to address the Brotherhood in 1920.

29. Bottom left. BRIDGE STREET, 1900. This was the site of the old horse fair but in this photograph the numerous tramlines hint at the demise of horse drawn transport. Here was the very heart of Victorian Bradford, one of the few open spaces in the city, the Town Hall Square. The elegant Mechanics' Institute building was erected in 1871 on the site of the Old Bowling Green Hotel. The Institute had provided part-time education and recreation for the artisans of industrial Bradford since 1832.

30. Right. TOWN HALL SQUARE, c1904. This is also part of the Mechanics' Institute building at the junction of Tyrrel Street (extreme left) and Manchester Road (front). This fine block also housed the Provincial Building Society. Queues for trams (centre) only became a feature of Bradford streets after the introduction of electric traction in 1898. Hitherto there were no official 'stops'.

31. Left. BOLTON WOODS QUARRY, c1910. In 1853 two working men, John Holmes and Thomas Dawson came to an agreement with Mr. Barton of Bolton Hall, concerning the quarrying of stone at Bolton Woods. It was the beginning of a very lucrative business, for the millowners of the West Riding were demanding fine quality ashlar for their multistorey mills and warehouses. The fine sandstone from Gaisby was used in many of Bradford's public and commercial buildings as well as those of other cities and ports throughout Britain. In this photograph the best stone (up to ten feet thick) is being cut by Waterhouse, Denbigh & Company subsequent owners of the Bolton Woods quarries.

32. Top right. OLD INFIRMARY. This is the dispensary entrance to the Old Infirmary in Westgate. The dispensary itself was opened in 1873 but the main building of the Infirmary was opened for in-patients in 1843 and was considerably extended twenty years later. The mock Tudor style of the original building was followed in all subsequent extensions including a new wing in 1885. Twelve years later Queen Victoria gave permission for the hospital to be named the Bradford Royal Infirmary.

33. Bottom right. LISTER PARK, 1914. On the condition that they would never sell more than fourteen acres, the Bradford Corporation purchased Manningham Hall and its fifty three acre estate from S. C. Lister in 1872. Lister Park, as it became, was one of Bradford's most popular recreational centres. The brass bands of the chapels, temperance league and the mills went through their full repertoires each Saturday and Sunday afternoons. As children rolled on the grassy slopes, young couples spooned dreamily past and some old men slept, many listened intently.

34. Left. THEATRE ROYAL, 1905. The theatre opened Boxing Day 1864 as the Royal Alexandra, as there was already a Theatre Royal in Duke Street. It finally took that name in 1868 when its reputation soared under the managership of Charles Rice. Although more famous for its pantomimes, many of the prominent Victorian stage names walked the theatre's boards. Lily Langtry appeared for a week in 1882, the fact that the Prince of Wales was opening the Bradford Technical College the same week was perhaps coincidental! The theatre was well known for its link with the death of Henry Irving who fell ill in the theatre whilst playing 'Becket' and died shortly afterwards.

35. Top right. VICTORIA SQUARE, 1920. Although Queen Victoria's statue dominates this view, the photograph includes the Prince's Theatre built by William Morgan and opened 17th April 1876. It was never able to compete with the Theatre Royal and in the 1880's was used as the Salvation Army Barracks. It was run as a melodrama house by Mr. Pullan in the 1890s. Under Francis Laidler the theatre competed with the Theatre Royal until Laidler purchased the latter for £40,000 in 1920 and converted it to a cinema the following year. The Prince's introduced repertory in 1931 and finally closed its doors in April 1961.

36. Bottom right. PARISH CHURCH, NORTH SIDE, c1900. In this photograph the mills, warehouses and operatives' cottages of industrial Bradford surround the town's ancient parish church and its graveyard. This is the third church built on this site. The first is said to date from the seventh century. A Norman church built 1200 A.D. was destroyed by the Scots almost a century later. The tower, which served Bradfordians well during the civil war, was added at the beginning of the sixteenth century. Under Dr. Scoresby and Dr. Burnet the interior of the church was completely transformed to provide its present imposing grandeur. It became a cathedral in 1918.

37. Left. BILL POSTER, c1890. Hoardings, like this one in Buttershaw, were a common feature of street culture before the First War. In town centres, gable ends were smothered by numerous advertisements for theatres, boot polish, liver pills etc. Such hoardings were a great help to many children of the lower classes in shaking off their illiteracy. They brought a humour and vitality to the dark and grimy bulks of Victorian architecture, and to the monotony of urban thoroughfares.

38. Right. MIDLAND STATION & HOTEL, 1906. When opened in March 1890, the Midland Station and Hotel ranked as one of the leading railway centres in the country. The scheme had first been mooted in 1874 but railway revenues would not permit the immediate construction of such an ambitious project. It took five years to build and cost over a million pounds. The station had six platforms, well equipped rooms and was lit by electricity throughout. It was directly linked to the hotel whose main entrance was in Kirkgate. The five storey hotel had initially sixty bedrooms, all impressively furnished.

39. Top left. FORSTER SQUARE c1910. This photograph is dominated by the statue of Richard Oastler, the 'Factory King'. It was unveiled in May 1869 by the 7th Earl of Shaftesbury. The bronze figures of Oastler and the two factory children moved Margaret McMillan as she stepped out of the railway station on her first visit to Bradford. In front of the church is the Post Office building erected in 1883.

BRADFORD CITY ENGLISH CUP TEAM.

O'ROURKE (Sec.).   ROBINSON.   CAMPBELL.   MELLORS.   TAYLOR.   HARPER (Trainer).

40. Bottom left. BRADFORD CITY, CUP-WINNERS 1911. This success came in only the eighth season of the club's existence, having been promoted from Division Two in 1908. Almost 40,000 spectators paid their sixpences to watch City beat Burnley in the quarter-final at Valley Parade. A surprise 3-0 victory over Blackburn Rovers gave them a place in the final against cup favourites Newcastle United. Supporters from eleven excursion trains were disappointed by a goalless draw at Crystal Palace. The replay at Old Trafford the following Wednesday enabled ten thousand Bradfordians to see their team (including eight Scots) beat Newcastle by a Jimmy Spiers header.

41. Left. SWAN ARCADE, 1900. Built on the site of the Old White Swan Inn, the arcade was designed by the architects Milnes & France and was completed in 1877. It fronted Market Street, Charles Street and Brook Street and its imposing archways and iron gates made many people think that it was private property in the early days. Its palatial accommodation included forty-four shops, a similar number of offices and numerous market rooms and warehouses.

42. Top left. A BRADFORD FEEDING CENTRE, 1908. School meals had been given to the necessitous poor in Bradford, on a voluntary basis, long before the Provision of Meals Act in 1906. The newly formed Bradford Education Committee had sought permission from the Board of Education to provide school meals from public funds in 1903. By autumn 1907 Bradford had its own central kitchen at Green Lane School. From there a special wagon delivered meals to a number of dining centres throughout the city. This photograph shows patient and hungry children at the White Abbey centre in 1908. It is thought that the supervisor is headteacher of Green Lane Elementary School, Jonathan Priestley, father of J. B. Priestley.

43. Bottom left. THE INFANT CLINIC. The municipal health department took over the post-natal work of various voluntary organisations in 1910. A clinic was opened in 1912 with every possible convenience. Young mothers could obtain drugs cheaply and also receive advice on the feeding, treatment and clothing of their babies. Guidance at this early stage helped to prevent many of the possible physical defects in later years.

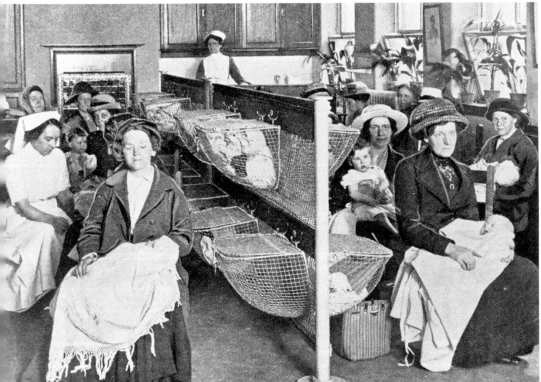

44. Right. A BRADFORD NANNY. 1901. Lister Park was a favourite spot for nursemaids and their charges from the Hallfield and Thorncliff estates and the many fine magnificent residences along Manningham Lane.

45. Left. THE BRADFORD INQUISITION? No! Just physical training in a Bradford elementary school in 1920. In 1909 the Board of Education issued a syllabus for physical exercise in elementary schools. Bradford schools quickly took up this scheme of free standing exercises in the roughly surfaced play grounds which were not always conducive to good physical training lessons. Ten years later the syllabus was extended to include games and running and jumping activities. At the same time secondary schools were providing gymnasium apparatus for their pupils.

46. Right. STREET CUTLER, c1890. A familiar sight in Bradford's streets before the First War, the knife and scissors grinder. An immaculately turned out young man awaits his mother's best carving knife!

T. MASTERSON
WORKING
CUTLER

ALL KINDS OF CUTLERY
GROUND & SET

47. TYRREL STREET, c1908. If the wind was in the right direction one could catch the aroma of freshly ground coffee from Collinson's on every day of the week except Sunday. The fascinating shop window, with its numerous blends of coffee and oriental teas, attracted many a passer-by and even tempted them inside to the delights of coffee and cakes, and even a three piece orchestra. The 129 tram on the busy Thornton Road service is one of the municipal steam trams first introduced in 1882 but superseded by electric traction after 1898.

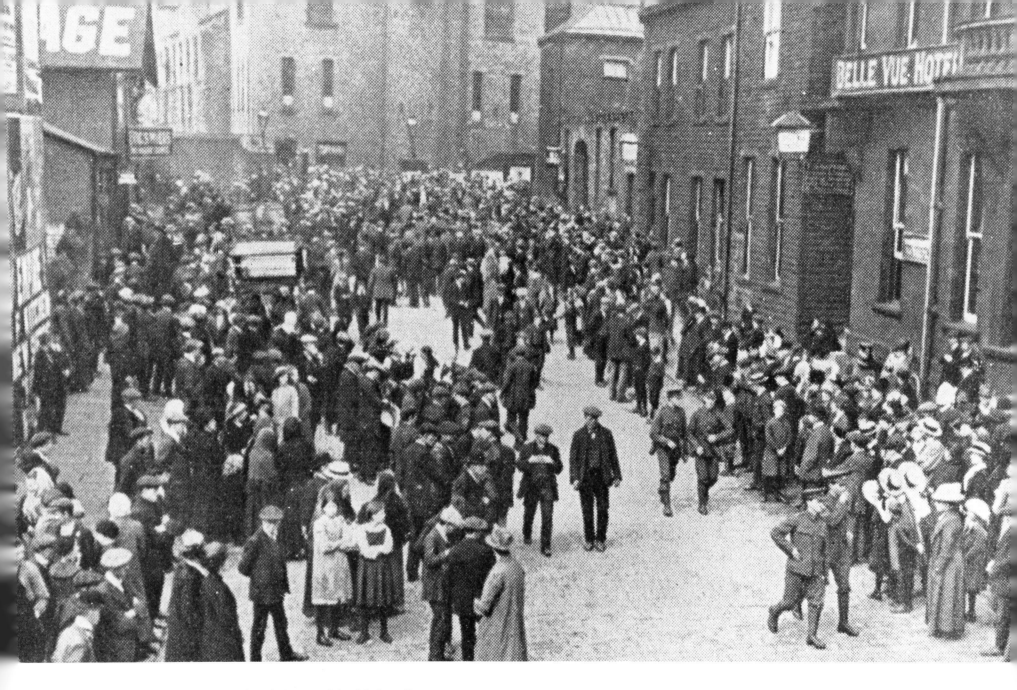

48. BRADFORD & MOBILIZATION, 1914. The 6th Battalion
West Yorkshire Regiment was mobilised on August 4th 1914. Four
days later a thousand men had responded to form E635 and were
assembled at Belle Vue Barracks. Here, outside the barracks, the
news breaks of the declaration of war.

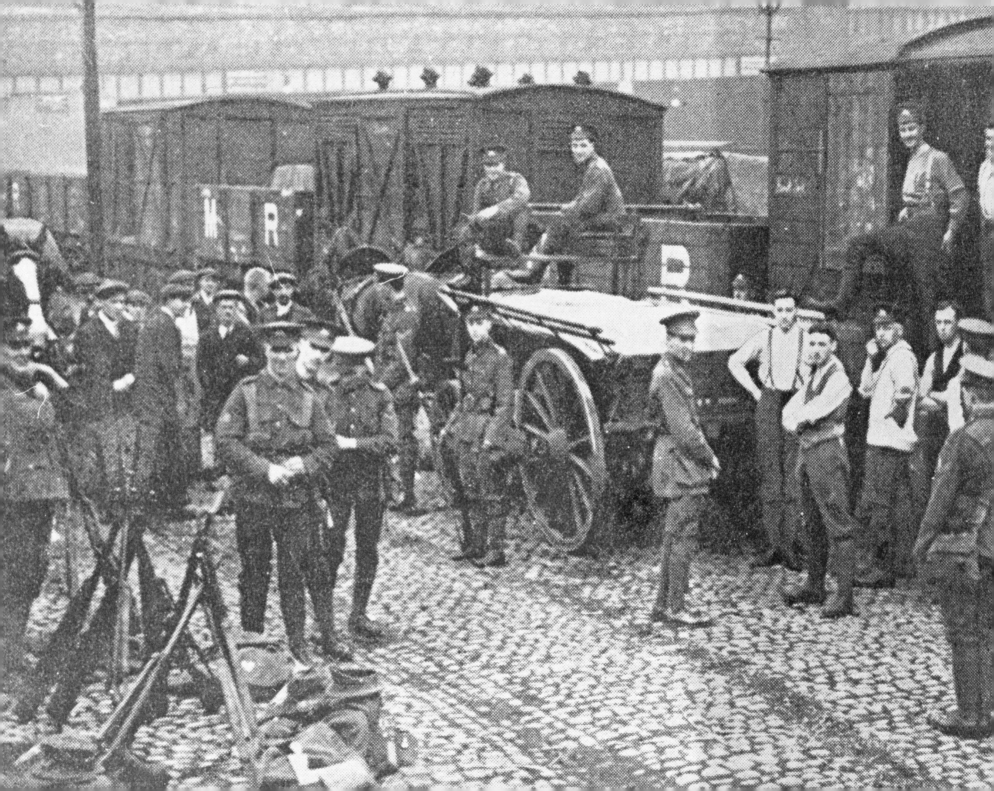

49. Left. THE TROOPS DEPART. On the 11th August the battalion left the barracks early in the morning. The march to the Midland Railway Station was viewed by solitary workers; there was no cheering, no acclaim.

50. Top right. DARLEY STREET. This district was originally part of the manorial estate, that is the gardens, orchards and rockery. It is thought to have been named after Darley Hall, seat of the manor lord. It had a reputation in 1900 for being the city's fashionable thoroughfare.

51. Bottom right. MANNINGHAM LANE & NORTH PARADE c1904. With the demolition of Christ Church in 1878, Darley Street was carried through to North Parade which had been given its name fifty years before. At Fountain Street, North Parade merged with Manningham Lane which was the chief promenade of the town, particularly since the opening of Lister Park.

The Yorkshire Penny Bank, built in 1895, commands the centre of the photograph.

52. Top left. MARKET STREET 1910. Formerly known as New Street, it was completely transformed by the civic rebuilding programme after 1860. The regular Italianate style of the buildings from Bank Street to the Town Hall was dominated by the elegant Venetian Gothic style of the Exchange, left of centre of the photograph. Beneath that building was the stained glass palace of Blake's drinking house and restaurant. On the immediate left can be seen a corner of Brown & Muff's lavish emporium opened in 1871, and for many years the finest and largest of its kind in the West Riding.

53. Bottom left. MARKET STREET. Another view of Market Street taken from the other end.

54. Right. WESTGATE 1920. Another of Bradford's original highways, Westgate's status as a residential area diminished as the town expanded after 1820. This view from the top of Ivegate is dominated by the Central Coffee Tavern and Hotel, formerly Manoah Rhodes, jewellers. Numerous public houses including the Pack Horse, Adelphi, Boy & Barrel and Star Inn were a feature of higher Westgate. On the left is Mr. A. Altham's tea shop renowned for free gifts of teapots, flowerstands and workboxes.

55 & 56. Left. CHARLES STREET AND BARKEREND ROAD. Two contrasting minor Bradford highways, Charles Street (above) dominated by the gloomy and oppressive warehouse blocks. Below, the more traditional Bradford street of Barkerend Road with its diminutive cottages and the ancient Paper Hall.

57. Right. WORK PEOPLE'S HOUSING. Even when the town was municipalised in 1847 the abuses perpetrated in the name of housebuilding continued for three decades. Hasty improvisation, in the form of back to back cottages, discounted any possibility of controlled planning. As late as 1921, the city had almost 41,000 back to back houses (54.4 per cent of total dwellings) and 3,700 of them were unfit for human habitation. The post war demand for accommodation ensured that most of them were lived in. Only after the war was a programme of standardised municipal housing commenced.

58. PRIVY MIDDENS. At the end of the nineteenth century a large proportion of working people in Bradford lived in accommodation like this, offering one room upstairs, one down and a windowless cellar. At the rear of the house (usually back to back) the privy midden, for every kind of refuse, served as many as four households. Opening the ashpit doors, the night soil men shovelled the refuse into the cobbled yards and into carts. The mess and stench they left behind was only cleaned the next day by the swilling and scrubbing of overworked housewives.

59. EVICTION. A familiar scene in Bradford streets before the First War. Deserted by the father, a family like this was not many weeks from total destitution and the workhouse. In most cases mothers, aged before their time with continuous child bearing, were too dependent to become 'bread-winners' overnight. Many were ignorant, not only of wordly matters but of personal hygiene and even the rudiments of babycare.

60. Top left. READING ROOM, BRADFORD LIBRARY 1922. For the ranks of the unemployed in the inter-war years Bradford Library's reading room in Darley Street was a favourite haunt. The city's first library had opened in Tyrrel Street in 1872. Six years later it transferred to new premises in the Kirkgate Market precinct. Within a decade this accommodation was inadequate but there was no futher move until 1966.

61. Bottom left. RAWSON PLACE MARKET. c1920. The butcher's portion was opened on 13th November 1875 and the extension to John Street completed thirty years later. The total cost was over £98,000 and provided 74 stalls and shops.

The Author: Gary Firth, who has lived all his life in mid-Airedale, was educated at Bingley Grammar School and Leeds University where he obtained his B.A. in 1968. He secured his doctorate from the University of Bradford in 1974 while teaching history in Bradford secondary schools. He is at present a lecturer in history at Bingley College, and also teaches local history for adult classes.

Dr. Firth's earlier book *Bingley History Trail,* also published by Hendon Publishing, is still in print.